SWITZERLAND

A PICTURE BOOK TO REMEMBER HER BY

Designed by
DAVID GIBBON

Produced by
TED SMART

CRESCENT

INTRODUCTION

Switzerland is one of the smallest countries in the world and it has often been called 'the roof of Europe' because of its mountainous terrain. It is also known as a country of infinite variety and character with a long tradition of hospitality.

The country is made up of a confederation of twenty-two states, or cantons, three of which have been subdivided. Each canton has its own local government which, in turn, is responsible to the federal government in the capital, Berne.

Switzerland has no single language. Its inhabitants speak a German dialect in the north, French and Italian in the south and a curious, ancient language known as Romansch in some parts of the east.

Since 1815, Switzerland, tired of the bloodshed of wars, has maintained a policy of neutrality. Today, therefore, having escaped the devastation of two world wars, her landscape remains unscarred and her historic buildings stand intact.

Being a landlocked country means that Switzerland does not have the attraction of a sea coast but she has, instead, magnificent mountains, lakes, forests, fairy-tale villages and impressive towns and cities.

The Alps and the Jura mountains, for so long a barrier, so far as the Swiss were concerned, were 'discovered' by the British, whose enthusiasm for climbing was unsurpassed. By the end of the 19th century they had climbed almost every peak – often without suitable equipment.

After establishing the sport of mountaineering, the British went on to popularize skiing and, after reading Sir Arthur Conan Doyle's account of a Swiss ski journey which was published in 1914, vast numbers of Britons visited the snow-covered slopes of Switzerland. Today there are over 1,200 ski lifts, cable cars and funicular railways, and resorts such as Zermatt, Davos, Gstaad and St. Moritz attract thousands of visitors. St. Moritz is regarded as the most luxurious and opulent centre, catering for the rich from all over the world and it is said that there is more activity to be seen in the streets than on the actual ski runs! It was here that, in 1884, the first artificial toboggan run, the famous Cresta, was constructed and it still presents one of the greatest challenges in sport.

Ice-skating, curling, hang-gliding, golf and tennis – in Switzerland there is something to suit every taste. Mountaineers of all nationalities continue to climb such hazardous peaks as the Eiger and the Matterhorn, for in many respects the Alps remain unrivalled in the large number and variety of climbs that are available, the quality of the rock and the beautiful views.

Tourism continues to be one of Switzerland's most important industries – and not only for winter sports enthusiasts. In late spring and summer, when much of the snow has melted, the valleys and lower slopes of the mountains are covered with lush, new grass and the vivid colours of alpine flowers. The air rings with the sound of bells as the cows are taken up the mountain slopes to their summer pastures. From these rich feeding grounds the cows produce the milk for the distinctive cheeses and delicious chocolate for which the Swiss are so famous.

Due to the high cost of transportation, many of Switzerland's manufacturing industries are ones that require skilled labour producing commodities of high value and small bulk. The most obvious example is that of watch-making – an industry in which Switzerland still reigns supreme. Great care is taken in the making and assembling of fine watch parts, so that the finished article lives up to its renowned reputation.

Watch-making is carried out both in factories and in the homes of individual craftsmen. Geneva, a city that spreads out around one end of Lake Geneva, is considered to be the world's leading watch-making and selling centre. It is also the home of the International Red Cross Society and the European Headquarters of the United Nations.

At the other end of the lake from Geneva is Montreux, a favourite winter resort. The famous castle of Chillon is close by, on an island just a few yards from the shore. Built in the 13th century, Chillon was a state prison for many years and it was immortalised by the poet Byron in his poem "The Prisoner of Chillon".

Lake Geneva itself is partly in Switzerland and partly in France. On the Swiss side are gentle, rolling hills covered with vineyards, backed by the great peaks of the Bernese Oberland. On the opposite side are the French Alps, dominated by Mont Blanc, at 15,781 feet the highest mountain in Europe.

Although Berne is the capital, Zurich is the largest city in Switzerland and it is situated at the northern end of the long, crescent-shaped lake that bears its name. The city has many factories but, due to all their energy requirements being met by electricity, they produce no smoke. The electricity comes from the many hydro-electric power stations that take full advantage of the country's fast-flowing rivers and waterfalls. The resultant clean air is one of Switzerland's most precious assets.

The heart of historic Switzerland is considered to be Lucerne, a prosperous and sophisticated city close to the legendary country of William Tell. It still has many buildings dating back to the 15th and 16th centuries and is particularly well-known for its delightful, covered wooden bridges. The most famous landmark, however, is the huge Lion of Lucerne which commemorates the heroic defence of the Tuileries by the Swiss Guard during the French Revolution of 1792, when they were trying to protect King Louis XVI.

Nestling between two more of Switzerland's jewel-like lakes, Thun and Brienz, is Interlaken. From here it is possible to take an excursion to the Jungfrau, on Europe's highest railroad. The Jungfrau terminus is at 11,333 feet, where the air is rarefied but the views are breathtaking. Not only can the Jungfrau peak be seen but also the ten mile long Aletsch Glacier, the peaks of Mönch and Eiger and, on a clear day, the Jura, the Vosges and even the Black Forest.

Left. The awe-inspiring majesty of the Matterhorn reflected in the Riffelsee.

Founded in 1157, Fribourg *left* is one of the loveliest towns in Switzerland. The River Saane flows through Fribourg and is crossed by some remarkably fine bridges, such as the Berne Bridge *right*.

A typical example *below* of the beautiful countryside that lies all around Fribourg.

An excellent example of a Roman Amphitheatre may be seen at Avenches *right*.

Colourful pots of geraniums and the distinctive red and white flags of Switzerland add splashes of colour to the striking picture of the Berne Gate in Murten *centre right*.

A solitary swan enjoys the tranquillity of the Lac de Joux *overleaf*.

One of the loveliest lakes in Switzerland is Lake Geneva. On its shores is the Tour de Marsens *left* and the famous Chateau du Chillon *below right* which in fact stands on a tiny island only ten yards from the shore and is reached by crossing a wooden bridge.

Spring flowers bloom in profusion *below* on the mountain-slopes above the lake.

Just a few miles from Lake Geneva, in the Rhône Valley, is Aigle, a prosperous wine-growing town with an imposing castle *right*.

Geneva *overleaf* is a truly international city and the European headquarters of the United Nations. The huge fountain known as the Jet d'Eau reaches a height of just over 400 feet and can be seen for many miles.

Small boats lie peacefully in the still waters of Lake Geneva near Clarens *left*.

Above the town of Vevey stands the Castle of Blonay *bottom left* which affords wonderful views of the surrounding countryside.

Zurich is Switzerland's most economically important city. Among its fine buildings is the Grossmünster Cathedral *below and centre right*.

Many of Zurich's buildings occupy outstanding positions on the edge of Lake Zurich *top right*

On a small peninsula jutting out into Lake Zurich is the charming old town of Rapperswil, with its pretty harbour *right*.

Like many Swiss cities, Zurich looks equally impressive at night *overleaf*.

Einsiedeln *left and centre left* was one of the first places in Switzerland to be visited by the early Christian missionaries. The remains of an ancient Benedictine Abbey, founded in 947 can still be seen there.

St Gallen *above and left* is considered to be Switzerland's most historic town. It also grew up around a Benedictine Abbey and was famous as a centre of learning in the 8th to 10th centuries.

The magnificently decorated building *right* is just one of the many beautiful buildings in the little town of Schwyz, which gave its name to Switzerland.

SCHLACHT
MORGARTEN
1315

WALTHER FÜ...

A breathtaking view of the interior of the Monastic church at Einsiedeln *right* and the magnificent ceiling paintings and elegant organ *below* of the cathedral at St Gallen.

Close to the spectacular Rhine Falls is the attractive town of Schaffhausen *above left*. It is dominated by the 16th century Munot, a completely round fortress 118 feet high with walls 16 feet thick, connected to the old town by a covered passageway.

The old town of Laufen *left* commands a fine position on the river bank in the midst of some exceptionally fine countryside.

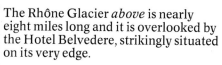

The Rhône Glacier *above* is nearly eight miles long and it is overlooked by the Hotel Belvedere, strikingly situated on its very edge.

The Grimsel Pass *left and above right* connects the Valley of the Rhône with the Bernese Oberland and is one of the grandest and most frequented Alpine passes.

Engelberg *centre right* is a well-known mountaineering centre and Andermatt *right and overleaf* is a compact village and winter sports resort that is also popular in summer, when the valley is green and peaceful.

Another popular Swiss holiday resort in Gersau *left* which has a most unusual history. For five centuries it declared itself an independent state – undoubtedly the smallest in Europe – if not the world.

Above. A tranquil scene near Burgenstock.

Lucerne is situated on both sides of the River Reuss, where it flows out of Lake Lucerne and it is dominated by Mount Pilatus, the second highest peak in the Canton. On the right bank of the Reuss is the old quarter of the town, known as Gross-stadt *left and right.*

Crossing the river diagonally is the quaint old Kapellbrücke *left and centre right,* a roofed, wooden bridge that is one of the most characteristic features of Lucerne. The picturesque Water Tower, at the southern end of the bridge, is possibly the oldest building in the town.

Above. A gaily decorated shopping street.

Lake Lucerne *right* has great scenic beauty and is popular for recreational purposes.

Berne, the capital of the Swiss Federation, is attractively situated on the River Aare. Several high bridges connect the old town with the modern quarters on the river's right bank. Many of its streets are flanked by arcades known as Lauben *above right* and the city is renowned for its numerous old fountains. The Kramgasse *above left* has a statue of the heraldic bear of Berne – the city's symbol – wearing armour and carrying a banner. *Left* are some of the attractive riverside buildings and *right* is the Federal Building of the Swiss Parliament.

Murren *left* is superbly situated at the top of the precipices above the Lauterbrunnen Valley and is a favourite ski resort.

To the north of Mürren is the village of Wengen *below*, which is also very popular with winter sports enthusiasts.

One of the highest peaks in the Alps is the Mönch *right* which rises to 13,448 feet above sea level.

Skiing is the most popular winter sport in
Switzerland. The superb facilities, well-kept runs,
numerous chair lifts and cable cars are unmatched
anywhere in the world. In addition, high resorts such
as St Moritz and Gstaad have guaranteed snow
conditions, good hotels and lively night life – or
après-ski. Even for the non-skier, however, just as
much pleasure can be derived from simply playing in,
and enjoying, the crisp, white snow, sunbathing or
travelling the easy way, in a snowmobile *overleaf*.

Grindelwald *above and far right* is an enchanting village occupying a sunny and sheltered situation. Its chief attractions are the majestic Wetterhorn, Mettenberg and Eiger *right*, which afford some of the best climbs in the whole of Switzerland.

The rugged, mountainous landscape of the Bernese Oberland is pictured *left*.

Dairy cows *above left* enjoy the rich grass in a field near Interlaken *left*. Commanding outstanding views of the Jungfrau, in addition to the Eiger and the Monch, is the delightful town of Thun *above*. The cool, green waters of the Lungernsee *top right* store water for a hydro-electric power station. In the foreground are the timber-built chalets of the village of Lungern. The picture *centre right* features the rustic charm of a water wheel in a small village in the Bernese Oberland and the medieval grandeur of Oberhofen Castle on Lake Thun is shown *right*.

Overleaf. The small harbour of the town of Spiez on Lake Thun.

The unmistakable shape of the Matterhorn towers majestically over the surrounding countryside. First climbed by Edward Whymper in 1865, the 14,782 ft mountain lies on the Swiss-Italian border south-west of the resort of Zermatt. This angular Alpine peak continues to be a challenge to enthusiastic climbers of every nationality.

Overleaf left is pictured Les Haudères mountain, 4,710 ft, and the Dent Blanches.
The vibrant colours of autumn leaves *overleaf right* contrast strikingly with the snow-covered peaks at Grachen.

The sparkling, frosted countryside *above* was photographed near the fashionable winter sports resort of Gstaad *above left*, a favourite meeting place of the 'jet set'.

Verbier *left* commands magnificent views of the Grand Combin.

Skiers at Saas-Fee *above right*, a typical Alpine resort.

The old village of Saillon *right* in the beautiful Canton Valais.

Overleaf. The village of Mase, in the spectacular Val d'Hérens, Valais. Sleigh rides *pages 50 and 51* provide a relaxing way of viewing the outstanding scenery near Arosa.

Chur *left and bottom left* is one of the oldest towns in Switzerland and was first occupied by the Celts in 2000 B.C.

Davos *right* consists of two virtually united towns and Monstein *centre right* is a small village close to Davos.

Skiers *above* take advantage of the snow and fine weather near the smart resort of St Moritz and typical Swiss houses and a delightful church cluster together at Graubünden *right*.

Home of the famous Cresta Run is St Moritz *overleaf*, where the rich congregate to enjoy the winter sports.

A stunning view *pages 56 and 57* of Madulain village in Engadine Canton.

Lying partly in Switzerland and partly in Italy, Lake Lugano is renowned for its outstanding natural beauty. Lugano *left* is the largest town in Ticino Canton and enjoys more hours of sunshine than anywhere else in Switzerland.

Morcote *below*, a few miles south of Lugano, boasts a beautiful 13th century church *bottom left*, the Madonna del Sasso and a church of the same name *right* dominates the town of Locarno.

The two tiny villages *centre right and right* appear overwhelmed by their rugged surroundings.

At 6,000 ft and situated in lovely wooded countryside is the popular resort of Silvaplana *overleaf*, which looks out over the lake of the same name.

Close to Silvaplana is the peaceful Silsersee *pages 62 and 63*, seen here displaying the rich colours of autumn.

First published in Great Britain 1978 by Colour Library International Ltd.
© Illustrations: Colour Library International Ltd. Colour separations by La Cromolito, Milan, Italy.
Display and text filmsetting by Focus Photoset, London, England.
Printed and bound by SAGDOS - Brugherio (MI), Italy.
Published by Crescent Books, a division of Crown Publishers Inc.
Library of Congress Catalogue Card No. 78-60543
CRESCENT 1978